SPIRITS
REBELLIOUS

by

Khalil Gibran

TRANSLATED FROM THE ARABIC
BY ANTHONY RIZCALLAH FERRIS

Edited by MARTIN L. WOLF

THE WISDOM LIBRARY

a division of

PHILOSOPHICAL LIBRARY
New York

Distributed to the trade by
CITADEL PRESS, INC.
A subsidiary of Lyle Stuart, Inc.
120 Enterprise Ave., Secaucus, N.J. 07094

ISBN 0-8065-0364-5

Contents

Editor's Preface

Soon after publication of the original Arabic of *Spirits Rebellious* at the turn of the century, considerable agitation and intrigue developed. The book was publicly burned in the *Beirut* market place by furious church and state officials who adjudged it poisonous, and fiercely dangerous to the peace of the country. *Lebanon* was then suffering virtual slavery under oppressive Turkish rule.

Gibran's bitter denunciation of both religious and political injustice prevailing at the time, brought also his anticipated exile from the country and excommunication from the church, although his parents were staunch Maronites. It was the story *Khalil the Heretic,* in particular, which drove the Sultan and his Emirs into trepidation, and caused nervous authorities in the entire Middle and Near East to examine into their governments.

Gibran was quietly pursuing painting with his friend Rodin in *Paris* when he learned of the ceremonial destruction of his book, and he merely expressed the thought that it was excellent cause for the issuance of a second edition.

In 1908 his exile was remanded, and the church embraced him without conciliation on his part. A mourner who witnessed the Gibran funeral procession in 1931, states that the ecclesiastical pageantry of the event was beyond description. Hundreds of priests and religious leaders, representing every denomination under Eastern skies, were in solemn attendance. Included were Maronites, Catholics, Shiites, Protestants, Mohammedans, Greek Orthodox, Jews, Sunnites, Druzes, and others. And to render complete Gibran's restoration to the fold of religion, he was buried in the grotto of the Monastery of *Mar Sarkis* in *Bsherri,* his childhood church.

M. L. W.

Madame Rose Hanie

Miserable is the man who loves a woman and takes her for a wife, pouring at her feet the sweat of his skin and the blood of his body and the life of his heart, and placing in her hands the fruit of his toil and the revenue of his diligence; for when he slowly wakes up, he finds that the heart, which he endeavored to buy, is given away freely and in sincerity to another man for the enjoyment of its hidden secrets and deepest love. Miserable is the woman who arises from the inattentiveness and restlessness of youth and finds herself in the home of a man showering her with his glittering gold and precious gifts and according her all the honors and grace of lavish entertainment but unable to satisfy her soul with the heavenly wine which God pours from the eyes of a man into the heart of a woman.

I knew Rashid Bey Namaan since I was a youngster; he was a Lebanese, born and reared in the City of Beyrouth. Being a member of an old and rich family which preserved the tradition and glory of his ancestry, Rashid was fond of citing incidents that dealt mainly with the nobility of his forefathers. In his routine life he followed their beliefs and customs which, at that time, prevailed in the Middle East.

Rashid Bey Namaan was generous and good-hearted, but like many of the Syrians, looked only at the superficial things instead of reality. He never hearkened to the dictates of his heart, but busied himself in obeying the voices of his environment. He amused himself with shimmering objects that blinded his eyes and heart to life's secrets; his soul was diverted away from an understanding of the law of nature, and to a temporary self-gratification. He was one of those men who hastened to confess their love or disgust to the people, then regretted their impulsiveness when it was too late for recall. And then shame and ridicule befell them, instead of pardon or sanction.

These are the characteristics that prompted Rashid Bey Namaan to marry Rose Hanie far before her soul embraced his soul in the shadow of the true love that makes union a paradise.

*   *   *   *

After a few years of absence, I returned to the City of Beyrouth. As I went to visit Rashid Bey Namaan, I found him pale and thin. On his face one could see the spectre of bitter disappointment; his sorrowful eyes bespoke his crushed heart and melancholy soul. I was curious to find the cause for his miserable plight; however, I did not hesitate to ask for explanation and said, "What became of you, Rashid? Where is the radiant smile and the happy countenance that accompanied you since childhood? Has death taken away from you a dear friend? Or have the black nights stolen from you the gold you have amassed during the white days? In the name of friendship, tell me what is causing this sadness of heart and weakness of body?"

He looked at me ruefully, as if I had revived to

him some secluded images of beautiful days. With a distressed and faltering voice he responded, "When a person loses a friend, he consoles himself with the many other friends about him, and if he loses his gold, he meditates for a while and casts misfortune from his mind, especially when he finds himself healthy and still laden with ambition. But when a man loses the ease of his heart, where can he find comfort, and with what can he replace it? What mind can master it? When Death strikes close by, you will suffer. But when the day and night pass, you will feel the smooth touch of the soft fingers of Life; then you will smile and rejoice.

Destiny comes suddenly, bringing concern; she stares at you with horrible eyes and clutches you at the throat with sharp fingers and hurls you to the ground and tramples upon you with ironclad feet; then she laughs and walks away, but later regrets her actions and asks you through good fortune to forgive her. She stretches forth her silky hand and lifts you high and sings to you the Song of Hope and causes you to lose your cares. She

4

creates in you a new zest for confidence and ambition. If your lot in life is a beautiful bird that you love dearly, you gladly feed to him the seeds of your inner self, and make your heart his cage and your soul his nest. But while you are affectionately admiring him and looking upon him with the eyes of love, he escapes from your hands and flies very high; then he descends and enters into another cage and never comes back to you. What can you do? Where can you find patience and condolence? How can you revive your hopes and dreams? What power can still your turbulent heart?"

Having uttered these words with a choking voice and suffering spirit, Rashid Bey Namaan stood shaking like a reed between the north and south wind. He extended his hands as if to grasp something with his bent fingers and destroy it. His wrinkled face was livid, his eyes grew larger as he stared a few moments, and it seemed to him as if he saw a demon appearing from nonexistence to take him away; then he fixed his eyes on mine and his appearance suddenly changed; his anger was converted into keen suffering and distress, and he cried out saying, "It is the woman—the woman whom I rescued from between the deathly paws of poverty; I opened my coffers to her and made her envied by all women for the beautiful raiment and precious gems and magnificent carriages drawn by spirited horses; the woman whom my heart has loved and at whose feet I poured my affection; the woman, to whom I was a true friend, sincere companion and a faithful husband; the woman who betrayed me and departed me for another man to share with him destitution and partake his evil bread, kneaded with shame and mixed with disgrace. The woman I loved; the beautiful bird whom I fed, and to whom I made my heart a cage, and my soul a nest, has escaped from my hands and entered into another cage; that pure angel, who resided in the paradise of my affection and love, now appears to me as a horrible demon, descended into the darkness to suffer for her sin and cause me to suffer on earth for her crime."

He hid his face with his hands as if wanting to

protect himself from himself, and became silent for a moment. Then he sighed and said, "This is all I can tell you; please do not ask anything further. Do not make a crying voice of my calamity, but let it rather be mute misfortune; perhaps it will grow in silence and deaden me away so that I may rest at last with peace."

I rose with tears in my eyes and mercy in my heart, and silently bade him goodbye; my words had no power to console his wounded heart, and my knowledge had no torch to illuminate his gloomy self.

PART II

A few days thereafter I met Madame Rose Hanie for the first time, in a poor hovel, surrounded by flowers and trees. She had heard of me through Rashid Bey Namaan, the man whose heart she had crushed and stamped upon and left under the terrible hoofs of Life. As I looked at her beautiful bright eyes, and heard her sincere voice, I said to myself, "Can this be the sordid woman? Can this clear face hide an ugly soul and a criminal heart? Is this the unfaithful wife? Is this the woman of whom I have spoken evil and imagined as a serpent disguised in the form of a beautiful bird?" Then I whispered again to myself saying, "Is it this beautiful face that made Rashid Bey Namaan miserable? Haven't we heard that obvious beauty is the cause of many hidden distresses and deep suffering? Is not the beautiful moon, that inspires the poets, the same moon that angers the silence of the sea with a terrible roar?"

As we seated ourselves, Madame Hanie seemed to have heard and read my thoughts and wanted not to prolong my doubts. She leaned her beautiful head upon her hands and with a voice sweeter than the sound of the lyre, she said, "I have never met you, but I heard the echoes of your thoughts and dreams from the mouths of the people, and they convinced me that you are merciful and have understanding for the oppressed woman—the woman whose heart's secrets you have discovered and whose affections you have known. Allow me to reveal to you the full contents of my heart so

8

you may know that Rose Hanie never was an un-faithful woman.

I was scarcely eighteen years of age when fate let me to Rashid Bey Namaan, who was then forty years old. He fell in love with me, according to what the people say, and took me for a wife and put me in his magnificent home, placing at my disposal servants and maids and dressing me with expensive clothes and precious gems. He exhibited me as a strange rarity at the homes of his friends and family; he smiled with triumph when he saw his contemporaries looking upon me with surprise and admiration; he lifted his chin high with pride when he heard the ladies speak of me with praise and affection. But never could he hear the whispers, 'Is this the wife of Rashid Bey Namaan, or his adopted daughter?' And another one commenting, 'If he had married at the proper age, his first born would have been older than Rose Hanie.'

All that happened before my life had awak-ened from the deep swoon of youth, and before God inflamed my heart with the torch of love, and before the growth of the seeds of my affections. Yes, all this transpired during the time when I believed that real happiness came through beautiful clothes and magnificent mansions. When I woke up from the slumber of childhood, I felt the flames of sacred fire burning in my heart, and a spiritual hunger gnawing at my soul, making it suffer. When I opened my eyes, I found my wings moving to the right and left, trying to ascend into the spacious firmament of love, but shivering and dropping under the gusts of the shackles of laws that bound my body to a man before I knew the true meaning of that law. I felt all these things and knew that a woman's happiness does not come through man's glory and honor, nor through his generosity and affection, but through love that unites both of their hearts and affections, making them one member of life's body and one word upon the lips of God. When Truth showed herself to me, I found myself imprisoned by law in the mansion of Rashid Bey Namaan, like a thief stealing his bread and hiding in the dark and friendly corners of the night. I knew that every hour spent with him was a terrible lie written upon my fore-head with letters of fire before heaven and earth. I could not give him my love and affection in reward for his generosity and sincerity. I tried in vain to love him, but love is a power that makes our hearts, yet our hearts cannot make that power. I prayed and prayed in the silence of the night before God to create in the depths of my heart a spiritual attachment that would carry me closer to the man who had been chosen for me as a com-panion through life.

My prayers were not granted, because Love descends upon our souls by the will of God and not by the demand or the plea of the individual. Thus I remained for two years in the home of that man, envying the birds of the field their free-dom while my friends envied me my painful chains of gold. I was like a woman who is torn from her only child; like a lamenting heart, exist-ing without attachment; like an innocent victim of the severity of human law. I was close to death from spiritual thirst and hunger.

One dark day, as I looked behind the heavy

skies, I saw a gentle light pouring from the eyes of a man who was walking forlornly on the path of life; I closed my eyes to that light and said to myself, 'Oh, my soul, darkness of the grave is thy lot, do not be greedy for the light.' Then I heard a beautiful melody from heaven that revived my wounded heart with its purity, but I closed my ears and said, 'Oh, my soul, the cry of the abyss is thy lot, do not be greedy for heavenly songs.' I closed my eyes again so I could not see, and shut my ears so I could not hear, but my closed eyes still saw that gentle light, and my ears still heard that divine sound. I was frightened for the first time and felt like the beggar who found a precious jewel near the Emir's palace and could not pick it up on account of fear, or leave it because of poverty. I cried—a cry of a thirsty soul who sees a brook surrounded by wild beasts, and falls upon the ground waiting and watching fearfully."

Then she turned her eyes away from me as if she remembered the past that made her ashamed to face me, but she continued, "Those people who go back to eternity before they taste the sweetness of real life are unable to understand the meaning of a woman's suffering. Especially when she devotes her soul to a man she loves by the will of God, and her body to another whom she caresses by the enforcement of earthly law. It is a tragedy written with the woman's blood and tears which the man reads with ridicule because he cannot understand it; yet, if he does understand, his laughter will turn into scorn and blasphemy that act like fire upon her heart. It is a drama enacted by the black nights upon the stage of a woman's soul, whose body is tied up into a man, known to her as husband, ere she perceives God's meaning of marriage. She finds her soul hovering about the man whom she adores by all agencies of pure and true love and beauty. It is a terrible agony that began with the existence of weakness in a woman and the commencement of strength in a man. It will not end unless the days of slavery and superiority of the strong over the weak are abolished. It is a horrible war between the corrupt law of humanity and the sacred affections and holy purpose of the heart. In such a battlefield I was lying yesterday, but I gathered the remnants of my strength, and unchained my irons of cowardice, and untied my wings from the swaddles of weakness and arose into the spacious sky of love and freedom.

Today I am one with the man I love; he and I sprang out as one torch from the hand of God before the beginning of the world. There is no power under the sun that can take my happiness from me, because it emanated from two embraced spirits, engulfed by understanding, radiated by Love, and protected by heaven."

She looked at me as if she wanted to penetrate my heart with her eyes in order to discover the impression of her words upon me, and to hear the echo of her voice from within me; but I remained silent and she continued. Her voice was full of bitterness of memory and sweetness of sincerity and freedom when she said, "The people will tell you that Rose Hanie is an heretic and unfaithful woman who followed her desires by leaving the man who elated her into him and made her the elegance of his home. They will tell you that she is an adulteress and prostitute who destroyed with her filthy hand the wreath of a sacred marriage and replaced it with a besmirched union woven of the thorns of hell. She took off the garment of virtue and put on the cloak of sin and disgrace. They will tell you more than that, because the ghosts of their fathers are still living in their bodies. They are like the deserted caves of the mountains that echo voices whose meanings are not understood. They neither understand the law of God, nor comprehend the true intent of veritable religion, nor distinguish between a sinner and an innocent. They look only at the surface of objects without knowing their secrets. They pass their verdicts with ignorance, and judge with blindness, making the criminal and the innocent, the good and the bad, equal. Woe to those who prosecute and judge the people. . . .

In God's eyes I was unfaithful and an adulteress only while at the home of Rashid Bey Namaan, because he made me his wife according to the customs and traditions and by the force of haste, before heaven had made him mine in conformity with the spiritual law of Love and Affection. I was a sinner in the eyes of God and myself when I ate his bread and offered him my body in reward for his generosity. Now I am pure and clean because the law of Love has freed me and made me honorable and faithful. I ceased selling my body for shelter and my days for clothes. Yes, I was an adulteress and a criminal when the people viewed me as the most honorable and faithful wife; today I am pure and noble in spirit, but in their opinion I am polluted, for they judge the soul by the outcome of the body and measure the spirit by the standard of matter."

Then she looked through the window and pointed out with her right hand toward the city as if she had seen the ghosts of corruption and the shadow of shame among its magnificent buildings. She said pityingly, "Look at those majestic mansions and sublime palaces where hypocrisy resides; in those edifices and between their beautifully decorated walls resides Treason beside Putridity; under the ceiling painted with melted gold lives Falsehood beside Pretension. Notice those gorgeous homes that represent happiness, glory and domination; they are naught but caverns of misery and distress. They are plastered graves in which Treason of the weak woman hides behind her kohled eyes and crimsoned lips; in their corners selfishness exists, and the animality of man through his gold and silver rules supreme.

If those high and impregnable buildings scented the odor of hatred, deceit and corruption, they would have cracked and fallen. The poor villager looks upon those residences with tearful eyes, but when he finds that the hearts of the occupants are empty of that pure love that exists in the heart of his wife and fills its domain, he will smile and go back to his fields contented."

And she took hold of my hand and led me to the side of the window and said, "Come, I will show you the uneviled secrets of those people whose path I refused to follow. Look at that palace with giant columns. In it lives a rich man who inherited his gold from his father. After having led a life of filth and putrefaction, he married a woman about whom he knew nothing except that her father was one of the Sultan's dignitaries. As soon as the wedding trip was over he became disgusted and commenced associations with women who sell their bodies for pieces of silver. His wife was left alone in that palace like an empty bottle left by a drunkard. She cried and suffered for the first time; then she realized that her tears were more precious than her degenerate husband. Now she is busying herself in the love and devotion of a young man upon whom she showers her joyous hours, and into whose heart she pours her sincere love and affection.

Let me take you now to that gorgeous home surrounded by beautiful gardens. It is the home of a man who comes from a noble family which ruled the country for many generations, but whose standards, wealth, and prestige have declined due to their indulgence in mad spending and slothfulness. A few years ago this man married an ugly but rich woman. After he acquired her fortune, he ignored her completely and commenced devoting himself to an attractive young woman. His wife today is devoting her time to curling her hair, painting her lips and perfuming her body. She wears the most expensive clothes and hopes that some young man will smile and come to visit her, but it is all in vain, for she cannot succeed except in receiving a smile from her ugly self in the mirror.

Observe that big manor, encircled with marble statuary; it is the home of a beautiful woman who possesses strange character. When her first husband died, she inherited all of his money and estates; then she selected a man with a weak mind and feeble body and became his wife to protect herself from the evil tongues, and to use him as a shield for her abominations. She is now among her admirers like a bee that sucks the sweetest and most delicious flowers.

That beautiful home next to it was built by the greatest architect in the province; it belongs to a greedy and substantial man who devotes all of his time to amassing gold and grinding the faces of the poor. He has a wife of supernatural beauty, bodily and spiritually, but she is like the rest, a victim of early marriage. Her father committed a crime by giving her away to a man before she attained understanding age, placing on her neck the heavy yoke of corrupt marriage. She is thin and pale now, and cannot find an outlet for her imprisoned affection. She is sinking slowly and craving for death to free her from the mesh of slavery and deliver her from a man who spends his life gathering gold and cursing the hour he married a barren woman who could not bring him a child to carry on his name and inherit his money.

In that home among those orchards lives an ideal poet; he married an ignorant woman who ridicules his works because she cannot understand them, and laughs at his conduct because she cannot adjust herself to his sublime way of life. That poet found freedom from despair in his love for a married woman who appreciates his intelligence and inspires him by kindling in his heart the torch of affections, and revealing to him the most beautiful and eternal sayings by means of her charm and beauty."

Silence prevailed for a few moments, and Madame Hanie seated herself on a sofa by the window as if her soul were tired of roaming those quarters. Then she slowly continued, "These are the residences in which I refused to live; these are the graves in which I, too, was spiritually buried. Those people from whom I have freed myself are the ones who become attracted by the body and repelled by the spirit, and who know naught of Love and Beauty. The only mediator between them and God is God's pity for their ignorance of the law of God. I cannot judge, for I was one of them, but I sympathize with all my heart. I do not hate them, but I hate their surrender to weakness and falsehood. I have said all these things to show you the reality of people from whom I have escaped against their will. I was trying to explain to you the life of persons who speak every evil against me because I have lost their friendship and finally gained my own. I emerged from their dark dungeon and directed my eyes towards the light where sincerity, truth and justice prevail. They have exiled me now from their society and I am pleased, because humanity does not exile except the one whose noble spirit rebels against despotism and oppression. He who does not prefer exile to slavery is not free by any measure of freedom, truth and duty.

Yesterday I was like a tray containing all kinds of palatable food, and Rashid Bey Namaan never approached me unless he felt a need for that food; yet both of our souls remained far apart from us like two humble, dignified servants. I have tried to reconcile myself to what people call misfortune, but my spirit refused to spend all its life kneeling with me before a horrible idol erected by the dark ages and called LAW. I kept my chains until I heard Love calling me and saw my spirit preparing to embark. Then I broke them and walked out from Rashid Bey Namaan's home like a bird freed from his iron cage and leaving behind me all the gems, clothes and servants. I came to live with my beloved, for I knew that what I was doing was honest. Heaven does not want me to weep and suffer. Many times at night I prayed for dawn to come and when dawn came, I prayed for the day to be over. God does not want me to lead a miserable life, for He placed in the depths of my heart a desire for happiness; His glory rests in the happiness of my heart.

This is my story and this my protest before heaven and earth; this is what I sing and repeat while the people are closing their ears for fear of hearing me and leading their spirits into rebellion that would crumble the foundation of their quavering society.

This is the rough pathway I have carved until I reached the mountain peak of my happiness. Now if death comes to take me away, I will be more than willing to offer myself before the Supreme Throne of Heaven without fear or shame. I am ready for the day of judgment and my heart is white as the snow. I have obeyed the will of God in everything I have done and followed the call of my heart while listening to the angelic voice of heaven. This is my drama which the people of Beyrouth call 'A curse upon the lips of life,' and 'An ailment in the body of society.' But one day love will arouse their hearts like the sun rays that bring forth the flowers even from contaminated earth. One day the wayfarers will stop by my grave and greet the earth that enfolds my body and say, 'Here lies Rose Hanie who freed herself from the slavery of decayed human laws in order to comply with God's law of pure love. She turned her face toward the sun so she would not see the shadow of her body amongst the skulls and thorns.' "

* * * *

The door was opened and a man entered. His eyes were shining with magic rays and upon his lips appeared a wholesome smile. Madame Hanie rose, took the young man's arm and introduced him to me, then gave him my name with flattering words. I knew that he was the one for whose sake she denied the whole world and violated all earthly laws and customs.

As we sat down, silence controlled. Each one of us was engrossed in deep thought. One minute worthy of silence and respect had passed when I looked at the couple sitting side by side. I saw something I had never seen before, and realized instantly the meaning of Madame Hanie's story.

24

I comprehended the secret of her protest against the society which persecutes those who rebel against confining laws and customs before determining the cause for the rebellion. I saw one heavenly spirit before me, composed of two beautiful and united persons, in the midst of which stood the god of Love stretching his wings over them to protect them from evil tongues. I found a complete understanding emanating from two smiling faces, illuminated by sincerity and surrounded by virtue. For the first time in my life I found the phantom of happiness standing between a man and a woman, cursed by religion and opposed by the law. I rose and bade them goodbye and left that poor hovel which Affection had erected as an altar to Love and Understanding. I walked past the buildings which Madame Hanie pointed out to me. As I reached the end of these quarters I remembered Rashid Bey Namaan and meditated his miserable plight and said to myself, "He is oppressed; will heaven ever listen to him if he complains about Madame Hanie? Had that woman done wrong when she left him and followed the freedom of her heart? Or did he commit a crime by subduing her body in marriage before subduing her heart in love? Which of the two is the oppressed and which is the oppressor? Who is the criminal and who is the innocent?"

Then I resumed talking to myself after a few moments of deep thinking. "Many times deception had tempted woman to leave her husband and follow wealth, because her love for riches and beautiful raiment blinds her and leads her into shame. Was Madame Hanie deceitful when she left her rich husband's palace for a poor man's hut? Many times ignorance kills a woman's honor and revives her passion; she grows tired and leaves her husband, prompted by her desires, and follows a man to whom she lowers herself. Was Madame Hanie an ignorant woman following her physical desires when she declared publicly her independence and joined her beloved young man? She could have satisfied herself secretly while at her husband's home, for many men were willing to be the slaves of her beauty and martyrs of her love. Madame Hanie was a miserable woman. She sought only happiness, found it, and embraced it. This is the very truth which society disrespects." Then I whispered through the ether and inquired of myself, "Is it permissible for a woman to buy her happiness with her husband's misery?" And my soul added, "Is it lawful for a man to enslave his wife's affection when he realizes he will never possess it?"

*　　*　　*　　*

I continued walking and Madame Hanie's voice was still sounding in my ears when I reached the extreme end of the city. The sun was disappearing and silence ruled the fields and prairies while the birds commenced singing their evening prayers. I stood there meditating, and then I sighed and said, "Before the throne of Freedom, the trees rejoice with the frolicsome breeze and enjoy the rays of the sun and the beams of the moon. Through the ears of Freedom these birds whisper and around Freedom they flutter to the music of the brooks. Throughout the sky of Freedom these flowers breathe their fragrance and before Freedom's eyes they smile when dawn comes.

Everything on earth lives according to the law of nature, and from that law emerges the glory and joy of liberty; but man is denied this fortune, because he set for the God-given soul a limited and earthly law of his own. He made for himself strict rules. Man built a narrow and painful prison in which he secluded his affections and desires. He dug out a deep grave in which he buried his heart and its purpose. If an individual, through the dictates of his soul, declares his withdrawal from society and violates the law, his fellowmen will say he is a rebel worthy of exile, or an infamous creature worthy only of execution. Will man remain a slave of self-confinement until the end of the world? Or will he be freed by the passing of time and live in the Spirit for the Spirit? Will man insist upon staring downward and backward at the earth? Or will he turn his eyes toward the sun so he will not see the shadow of his body amongst the skulls and thorns?"

The Cry of the Graves

I

THE Emir walked into the court room and took the central chair while at his right and left sat the wise men of the country. The guards, armed with swords and spears, stood in attention, and the people who came to witness the trial rose and bowed ceremoniously to the Emir whose eyes emanated a power that revealed horror to their spirits and fear to their hearts. As the court came to order and the hour of judgment approached, the Emir raised his hand and shouted saying, "Bring forth the criminals singly and tell me what crimes they have committed." The prison door opened like the mouth of a ferocious yawning beast. In the obscure corners of the dungeon one could hear the echo of shackles rattling in unison with the moaning and lamentations of the prisoners. The spectators were eager to see the prey of Death emerging from the depths of that inferno. A few moments later, two soldiers came out leading a young man with his arms pinioned behind his back. His stern face bespoke nobility of spirit and strength of the heart. He was halted in the middle of the court room and the soldiers marched a few steps to the rear. The Emir stared at him steadily and said, "What crime has this man, who is proudly and triumphantly standing before me, committed?" One of the courtmen responded, "He is a murderer; yesterday he slew one of the Emir's officers who was on an important mission in the surrounding villages; he was still grasping the bloody sword when he was arrested." The Emir retorted with anger, "Return the man to the dark prison and tie him with heavy chains, and at dawn cut off his head with his own sword and throw his body in the woods so that the beasts may eat the flesh, and the air may carry its remindful odor into the noses of his family and friends." The youth was returned to prison while the people looked upon him with sorrowful eyes, for he was a young man in the spring of life.

The soldiers returned back again from the prison leading a young woman of natural and frail beauty. She looked pale and upon her face appeared the signs of oppression and disappointment. Her eyes were soaked with tears and her head was bent under the burden of grief. After eyeing her thoroughly, the Emir exclaimed, "And this emaciated woman, who is standing before me like the shadow beside a corpse, what has she done?" One of the soldiers answered him, saying, "She is an adulteress; last night her husband discovered her in the arms of another. After her lover escaped, her husband turned her over to the law." The Emir looked at her while she raised her face without expression, and he ordered, "Take her back to the dark room and stretch her upon a bed of thorns so she may remember the resting place which she polluted with her fault; give her vinegar mixed with gall to drink so she may remember the taste of those sweet kisses. At dawn drag her naked body outside the city and stone her. Let the wolves enjoy the tender meat of her body and the worms pierce her bones." As she walked back to the dark cell, the people looked upon her with sympathy and surprise. They were astonished with the Emir's justice and grieved over her fate. The soldiers reappeared, bringing with them a sad man with shaking knees and trembling like a tender sapling before the north wind. He looked powerless, sickly and frightened, and he was miserable and poor. The Emir stared at him loathfully and inquired, "And this filthy man, who is like dead amongst the living; what has he done?" One of the guards returned, "He is a thief who broke into the monastery and stole the sacred vases which the priests found under his garment when they arrested him."

As a hungry eagle who looks at a bird with broken wings, the Emir looked at him and said, "Take him back to the jail and chain him, and at dawn drag him into a lofty tree and hang him between heaven and earth so his sinful hands may perish and the members of his body may be turned into particles and scattered by the wind." As the thief stumbled back into the depths of the prison, the people commenced whispering one to another saying, "How dare such a weak and heretic man steal the sacred vases of the monastery?"

At this time the court adjourned and the Emir walked out accompanied by all his wise men, guarded by the soldiers, while the audience scattered and the place became empty except of the moaning and wailing of the prisoners. All this happened while I was standing there like a mirror before passing ghosts. I was meditating the laws, made by man for man, contemplating what the people call "justice," and engrossing myself with deep thoughts of the secrets of life. I tried to understand the meaning of the universe. I was dumbfounded in finding myself lost like a horizon that disappears beyond the cloud. As I left the place I said to myself, "The vegetable feeds upon the elements of the earth, the sheep eats the vegetable, the wolf preys upon the sheep, and the bull kills the wolf while the lion devours the bull; yet Death claims the lion. Is there any power that will overcome Death and make these brutalities an eternal justice? Is there a force that can convert all the ugly things into beautiful objects? Is there any might that can clutch with its hands all the elements of life and embrace them with joy as the sea joyfully engulfs all the brooks into its depths? Is there any power that can arrest the murdered and the murderer, the adulteress and the adulterer, the robber and the robbed, and bring them to a court loftier and more supreme than the court of the Emir?"

II

The next day I left the city for the fields where silence reveals to the soul that which the spirit desires, and where the pure sky kills the germs of despair, nursed in the city by the narrow streets and obscured places. When I reached the valley, I saw a flock of crows and vultures soaring and descending, filling the sky with cawing, whistling and rustling of the wings. As I proceeded I saw before me a corpse of a man hanged high in a tree, the body of a dead naked woman in the midst of a heap of stones, and a carcass of a youth with his head cut off and soaked with blood mixed with earth. It was a horrible sight that blinded my eyes with a thick, dark veil of sorrows. I looked in every direction and saw naught except the spectre of Death standing by those ghastly remains. Nothing could be heard except the wailing of non-existence, mingled with the cawing of crows hovering about the victims of human laws. Three human beings, who yesterday were in the lap of Life, today fell as victims to Death because they broke the rules of human society. When a man kills another man, the people say he is a murderer, but when the Emir kills him, the Emir is just. When a man robs a monastery, they say he is a thief, but when the Emir robs him of his life, the Emir is honorable. When a woman betrays her husband, they say she is an adulteress, but when the Emir makes her walk naked in the streets and stones her later, the Emir is noble. Shedding of blood is forbidden, but who made it lawful for the Emir? Stealing one's money is a crime, but taking away one's life is a noble act. Betrayal of

a husband may be an ugly deed, but stoning of living souls is a beautiful sight. Shall we meet evil
with evil and say this the Law? Shall we fight corruption with greater corruption and say this is the
Rule? Shall we conquer crimes with more crimes
and say this is Justice? Had not the Emir killed an
enemy in his past life? Had he not robbed his
weak subjects of money and property? Had he
not committed adultery? Was he infallible when
he killed the murderer and hanged the thief and
stoned the adulteress? Who are those who hanged
the thief in the tree? Are they angels descended
from heaven, or men looting and usurping? Who
cut off the murderer's head? Are they divine
prophets, or soldiers shedding blood wherever
they go? Who stoned that adulteress? Were they
virtuous hermits who came from their monasteries,
or humans who loved to commit atrocities with
glee, under the protection of ignorant Law? What
is Law? Who saw it coming with the sun from the
depths of heaven? What human saw the heart of
God and found its will or purpose? In what century did the angels walk among the people and

preach to them, saying, "Forbid the weak from enjoying life, and kill the outlaws with the sharp edge of the sword, and step upon the sinners with iron feet?"

As my mind suffered in this fashion, I heard a rustling of feet in the grass close by. I took heed and saw a young woman coming from behind the trees; she looked carefully in every direction before she approached the three carcasses that were there. As she glanced, she saw the youth's head that was cut off. She cried fearfully, knelt, and embraced it with her trembling arms; then she commenced shedding tears and touching the blood-matted, curly hair with her soft fingers, crying in a voice that came from the remnants of a shattered heart. She could bear the sight no longer. She dragged the body to a ditch and placed the head gently between the shoulders, covered the entire body with earth, and upon the grave she planted the sword with which the head of the young man had been cut off.

As she started to leave, I walked toward her. She trembled when she saw me, and her eyes were heavy with tears. She sighed and said, "Turn me over to the Emir if you wish; It is better for me to die and follow the one who saved my life from the grip of disgrace than to leave his corpse as food for the ferocious beasts." Then I responded, "Fear me not, poor girl, I have lamented the young man before you did. But tell me, how did he save you from the grip of disgrace?" She replied with a choking and fainting voice, "One of the Emir's officers came to our farm to collect the tax; when he saw me, he looked upon me as a wolf looks upon a lamb. He imposed on my father a heavy tax that even a rich man could not pay. He arrested me as a token to take to the Emir in ransom for the gold which my father was unable to give. I begged him to spare me, but he took no heed, for he had no mercy. Then I cried for help, and this young man, who is dead now, came to my help and saved me from a living death. The officer attempted to kill him, but this man took an old sword that was hanging on the wall of our home and stabbed him. He did not run away like a criminal, but stood by the dead officer until the law came and

38

took him into custody." Having uttered these words which would make any human heart bleed with sorrow, she turned her face and walked away.

In a few moments I saw a youth coming and hiding his face with a cloak. As he approached the corpse of the adulteress, he took off the garment and placed it upon her naked body. Then he drew a dagger from under the cloak and dug a pit in which he placed the dead girl with tenderness and care, and covered her with earth upon which he poured his tears. When he finished his task, he plucked some flowers and placed them reverently upon the grave. As he started to leave, I halted him saying, "What kin are you to this adulteress? And what prompted you to endanger your life by coming here to protect her naked body from the ferocious beasts?" When he stared at me, his sorrowful eyes bespoke his misery, and he said, "I am the unfortunate man for whose love she was stoned; I loved her and she loved me since childhood; we grew together; Love, whom we served and revered, was the lord of our hearts. Love joined both of us and embraced our souls. One day

I absented myself from the city, and upon my return I discovered that her father obliged her to marry a man she did not love. My life became a perpetual struggle, and all my days were converted into one long and dark night. I tried to be at peace with my heart, but my heart would not be still. Finally I went to see her secretly and my sole purpose was to have a glimpse of her beautiful eyes and hear the sound of her serene voice. When I reached her house I found her lonely, lamenting her unfortunate self. I sat by her; silence was our important conversation and virtue our companion. One hour of understanding quiet passed, when her husband entered. I cautioned him to contain himself but he dragged her with both hands into the street and cried out saying, "Come, come and see the adulteress and her lover!" All the neighbours rushed about and later the law came and took her to the Emir, but I was not touched by the soldiers. The ignorant Law and sodden customs punished the woman for her father's fault and pardoned the man."

Having thus spoken, the man turned toward the

city while I remained pondering the corpse of the thief hanging in that lofty tree and moving slightly every time the wind shook the branches, waiting for some one to bring him down and stretch him upon the bosom of the earth beside the Defender of Honor and Martyr of Love. An hour later, a frail and wretched woman appeared, crying. She stood before the hanged man and prayed reverently. Then she struggled up into the tree and gnawed with her teeth on the linen rope until it broke and the dead fell on the ground like a huge wet cloth; whereupon she came down, dug a grave, and buried the thief by the side of the other two victims. After covering him with earth, she took two pieces of wood and fashioned a cross and placed it over the head. When she turned her face to the city and started to depart, I stopped her saying, "What incited you to come and bury this thief?" She looked at me miserably and said, "He is my faithful husband and merciful companion; he is the father of my children—five young ones starving to death; the oldest is eight years of age, and the youngest is still nursing. My husband was not a thief, but a farmer working in the monastery's land, making our living on what little food the priests and monks gave him when he returned home at eventide. He had been farming for them since he was young, and when he became weak, they dismissed him, advising him to go back home and send his children to take his place as soon as they grew older. He begged them in the name of Jesus and the angels of heaven to let him stay, but they took no heed to his plea. They had no mercy on him nor on his starving children who were helplessly crying for food. He went to the city seeking employment, but in vain, for the rich did not employ except the strong and the healthy. Then he sat on the dusty street stretching his hand toward all who passed, begging and repeating the sad song of his defeat in life, while suffering from hunger and humiliation, but the people refused to help him, saying that lazy people did not deserve alms. One night, hunger gnawed painfully at our children, especially the youngest, who tried hopelessly to nurse on my dry breast. My husband's expression changed and he left the house under the cover of night. He entered the monastery's bin and carried out a bushel of wheat. As he emerged, the monks woke up from their slumber and arrested him after beating him mercilessly. At dawn they brought him to the Emir and complained that he came to the monastery to steal the golden vases of the altar. He was placed in prison and hanged the second day. He was trying to fill the stomachs of his little hungry ones with the wheat he had raised by his own labour, but the Emir killed him and used his flesh as food to fill the stomachs of the birds and the beasts." Having spoken in this manner, she left me alone in a sorrowful plight and departed.

*   *   *   *

I stood there before the graves like a speaker suffering wordlessness while trying to recite a eulogy. I was speechless, but my falling tears substituted for my words and spoke for my soul. My spirit rebelled when I attempted to meditate a while, because the soul is like a flower that folds its petals when dark comes, and breathes not its fra-

grance into the phantoms of the night. I felt as if
the earth that enfolded the victims of oppression
in that lonely place were filling my ears with sorrowful tunes of suffering souls, and inspiring me
to talk. I resorted to silence, but if the people
understood what silence reveals to them, they
would have been as close to God as the flowers of
the valleys. If the flames of my sighing soul had
touched the trees, they would have moved from
their places and marched like a strong army to
fight the Emir with their branches and tear down
the monastery upon the heads of those priests and
monks. I stood there watching, and felt that the
sweet feeling of mercy and the bitterness of sorrow were pouring from my heart upon the newly
dug graves—a grave of a young man who sacri-
ficed his life in defending a weak maiden, whose
life and honor he had saved from between the
paws and teeth of a savage human; a youth whose
head was cut off in reward for his bravery; and
his sword was planted upon his grave by the one
he saved, as a symbol of heroism before the face
of the sun that shines upon an empire laden with

stupidity and corruption. A grave of a young woman whose heart was inflamed with love before her body was taken by greed, usurped by lust, and stoned by tyranny. . . . She kept her faith until death; her lover placed flowers upon her grave to speak through their withering hours of those souls whom Love had selected and blessed among a people blinded by earthly substance and muted by ignorance. A grave of a miserable man, weakened by hard labour in the monastery's land, who asked for bread to feed his hungry little ones, and was refused. He resorted to begging, but the people took no heed. When his soul led him to restore a small part of the crop which he had raised and gathered, he was arrested and beaten to death. His poor widow erected a cross upon his head as a witness in the silence of the night before the stars of heaven to testify against those priests who converted the kind teaching of Christ into sharp swords by which they cut the people's necks and tore the bodies of the weak.

The sun disappeared behind the horizon as if tiring of the world's troubles and loathing the people's submission. At that moment the evening began to weave a delicate veil from the sinews of silence and spread it upon Nature's body. I stretched my hand toward the graves, pointing at their symbols, lifted my eyes toward heaven and cried out, "Oh, Bravery, this is your sword, buried now in the earth! Oh, Love, these are your flowers, scorched by fire! Oh, Lord Jesus, this is Thy Cross, submerged in the obscurity of the night!"

Khalil the Heretic

I

SHEIK ABBAS was looked upon as a prince by the people of a solitary village in North Lebanon. His mansion stood in the midst of those poor villagers' huts like a healthy giant amidst sickly dwarfs. He lived amid luxury while they pursued an existence of penury. They obeyed him and bowed reverently before him as he spoke to them. It seemed as though the power of mind had appointed him its official interpreter and spokesman. His anger would make them tremble and scatter like autumn leaves before a strong wind. If he were to slap one's face, it would be heresy on the individual's part to move or lift his head or make any attempt to discover why the blow had come. If he smiled at a man, the villagers would consider the person thus honoured as the most fortunate. The people's fear and surrender to Sheik Abbas were not due to weakness; however, their poverty and need of him had brought about this state of continual humiliation. Even the huts they lived in and the fields they cultivated were owned by Sheik Abbas who had inherited them from his ancestors.

The farming of the land and the sowing of the seeds and the gathering of wheat were all done under the supervision of the Sheik who, in reward for their toil, compensated them with a small portion of the crop which barely kept them from falling as victims of gnawing starvation.

Often many of them were in need of bread before the crop was reaped, and they came to Sheik Abbas and asked him with pouring tears to advance them a few piastres or a bushel of wheat, and the Sheik gladly granted their request for he knew that they would pay their debts doubly when harvest time came. Thus those people remained obligated all their lives, left a legacy of debts to their children and were submissive to their master whose anger they had always feared and whose friendship and good will they had constantly but unsuccessfully endeavoured to win.

II

Winter came and brought heavy snow and strong winds; the valleys and the fields became empty of all things except leafless trees which stood as spectres of death above the lifeless plains.

Having stored the products of the land in the Sheik's bins and filled his vases with the wine of the vineyards, the villagers retreated to their huts to spend a portion of their lives idling by the fireside and commemorating the glory of the past ages and relating to one another the tales of weary days and long nights.

The old year had just breathed its last into the grey sky. The night had arrived during which the New Year would be crowned and placed upon the throne of the Universe. The snow began to fall heavily and the whistling winds were racing from the lofty mountains down to the abyss and blowing the snow into heaps to be stored away in the valleys.

The trees were shaking under the heavy storms and the fields and knolls were covered with a white floor upon which Death was writing vague lines and effacing them. The mists stood as partitions between the scattered villages by the sides of the valleys. The lights that flickered through the windows of those wretched huts disappeared behind the thick veil of Nature's wrath.

Fear penetrated the fellahin's hearts and the animals stood by their mangers in the sheds, while the dogs were hiding in the corners. One could hear the voices of the screaming winds and thundering of the storms resounding from the depths of the valleys. It seemed as if Nature were enraged by the passing of the old year and trying to wrest revenge from those peaceful souls by fighting with weapons of cold and frost.

That night under the raging sky, a young man was attempting to walk the winding trail that connected Deir Kizhaya* with Sheik Abbas'

* One of the richest and most famous convents in Lebanon. Kizhaya is a Syriac word meaning "Paradise of Life." [Editor's note.]

village. The youth's limbs were numbed with cold, while pain and hunger usurped him of his strength. The black raiment he wore was bleached with the falling snow, as if he were shrouded in death before the hour of his death had come. He was struggling against the wind. His progress was difficult, and he took but a few steps forward with each effort. He called for help and then stood silent, shivering in the cold night. He had slim hope, withering between great despair and deep sorrow. He was like a bird with a broken wing, who fell in a stream whose whirlpools carried him down to the depths.

The young man continued walking and falling until his blood stopped circulating and he collapsed. He uttered a terrible sound . . . the voice of a soul who encountered the hollow face of Death . . . a voice of dying youth, weakened by man and trapped by nature . . . a voice of the love of existence in the space of nothingness.

III

On the north side of that village, in the midst
of the wind-torn fields, stood the solitary home of
a woman named Rachel, and her daughter Miriam who had not then attained the age of eighteen. Rachel was the widow of Samaan Ramy, who
was found slain six years earlier, but the law of
man did not find the murderer.

Like the rest of the Lebanese widows, Rachel
sustained life through long, hard work. During
the harvest season, she would look for ears of corn
left behind by others in the fields, and in Autumn
she gathered the remnants of some forgotten fruits
in the gardens. In Winter she spun wool and made
raiment for which she received a few piastres or a
bushel of grain. Miriam, her daughter, was a beautiful girl who shared with her mother the burden
of toil.

That bitter night the two women were sitting
by the fireplace whose warmth was weakened by
the frost and whose firebrands were buried beneath
the ashes. By their side was a flickering lamp that

sent its yellow, dimmed rays into the heart of darkness like prayer that sends phantoms of hope into the hearts of the sorrowful.

Midnight had come and they were listening to the wailing winds outside. Every now and then Miriam would get up, open the small transom and look toward the obscured sky, and then she would return to her chair worried and frightened by the raging elements. Suddenly Miriam started, as if she had awakened from a swoon of deep slumber. She looked anxiously toward her mother and said, "Did you hear that, Mother? Did you hear a voice calling for help?" The mother listened a moment and said, "I hear nothing except the crying wind, my daughter." Then Miriam exclaimed, "I heard a voice deeper than the thundering heaven and more sorrowful than the wailing of the tempest."

Having uttered these words, she stood up and opened the door and listened for a moment. Then she said, "I hear it again, Mother!" Rachel hurried toward the frail door and after a moment's hesitation she said, "And I hear it, too. Let us go and see."

She wrapped herself with a long robe, opened the door and walked out cautiously, while Miriam stood at the door, the wind blowing her long hair.

Having forced her way a short distance through the snow, Rachel stopped and shouted out, "Who is calling . . . where are you?" There was no answer; then she repeated the same words again and again, but she heard naught except thunder. Then she courageously advanced forward, looking in every direction. She had walked for some time, when she found some deep footprints upon the snow; she followed them fearfully and in a few moments found a human body lying before her on the snow, like a patch on a white dress. As she approached him and leaned his head over her knees, she felt his pulse that bespoke his slowing heart beats and his slim chance in life. She turned her face toward the hut and called, "Come, Miriam, come and help me, I have found him!" Miriam rushed out and followed her mother's footprints, while shivering with cold and trembling with fear. As she reached the place and saw the youth lying motionless, she cried with an aching voice. The mother put her hands under his armpits, calmed Miriam and said, "Fear not, for he is still living; hold the lower edge of his cloak and let us carry him home."

Confronted with the strong wind and heavy snow, the two women carried the youth and started toward the hut. As they reached the little haven, they laid him down by the fireplace. Rachel commenced rubbing his numbed hands and Miriam drying his hair with the end of her dress. The youth began to move after a few minutes. His eyelids quivered and he took a deep sigh—a sigh that brought the hope of his safety into the hearts of the merciful women. They removed his shoes and took off his black robe. Miriam looked at her mother and said, "Observe his raiment, Mother; these clothes are worn by the monks." After feeding the fire with a bundle of dry sticks, Rachel looked at her daughter with perplexity and said, "The monks do not leave their convent on such a terrible night." And Miriam inquired, "But he has no hair on his face; the monks wear beards." The mother gazed at him with eyes full of mercy and maternal love; then she turned to her daughter and said, "It makes no difference whether he is a monk or criminal; dry his feet well, my daughter." Rachel opened a closet, took from it a jar of wine and poured some in an earthenware bowl. Miriam held his head while the mother gave him some of it to stimulate his heart. As he sipped the wine he opened his eyes for the first time and gave his rescuers a sorrowful look mingled with tears of gratitude—the look of a human who felt the smooth touch of life after having been gripped in the sharp claws of death—a look of great hope after hope had died. Then he bent his head, and his lips trembled when he uttered the words, "May God bless both of you." Rachel placed her hand upon his shoulder and said, "Be calm, brother. Do not tire yourself with talking until you gain strength." And Miriam added, "Rest your head on this pillow, brother, and we will place you closer to the fire." Rachel refilled the bowl with wine and gave it to him. She looked at her daughter and said, "Hang his robe by the fire so it will dry." Having executed her mother's command, she returned and commenced looking at him mercifully, as if she wanted to help him by pouring into his heart all the warmth of her soul. Rachel brought two loaves of bread with some preserves and dry fruits; she sat by him and began to feed him small morsels, as a mother feeds her little child. At this time he felt stronger and sat up on the hearth mat while the red flames of fire reflected upon his sad face. His eyes brightened and he shook his head slowly, saying, "Mercy and cruelty are both wrestling in the human heart like the mad elements in the sky of this terrible night, but mercy shall overcome cruelty because it is divine, and the terror alone, of this night, shall pass away when daylight comes." Silence prevailed for a minute and then he added with a whispering voice, "A human hand drove me into desperation and a human hand rescued me; how severe man is, and how merciful man is!" And Rachel inquired, "How ventured you, brother, to leave the convent on such a terrible night, when even the beasts do not venture forth?"

The youth shut his eyes as if he wanted to restore his tears back into the depths of his heart, whence they came, and he said, "The animals have their caves, and the birds of the sky their nests, but the son of man has no place to rest his head." Rachel retorted, "That is what Jesus said about himself." And the young man resumed, "This is the answer for every man who wants to follow the Spirit and the Truth in this age of falsehood, hypocrisy and corruption."

After a few moments of contemplation, Rachel said, "But there are many comfortable rooms in the convent, and the coffers are full of gold, and all kinds of provisions. The sheds of the convent are stocked with fat calves and sheep; what made you leave such haven in this deathly night?" The youth sighed deeply and said, "I left that place because I hated it." And Rachel rejoined, "A monk in a convent is like a soldier in the battlefield who is required to obey the orders of his leader regardless of their nature. I heard that a man could not become a monk unless he did away with his will, his thought, his desires, and all that pertains to the mind. But a good head priest does not ask his monks

58

to do unreasonable things. How could the head priest of Deir Kizhaya ask you to give up your life to the storms and snow?" And he remarked, "In the opinion of the head priest, a man cannot become a monk unless he is blind and ignorant, senseless and dumb. I left the convent because I am a sensible man who can see, feel, and hear."

Miriam and Rachel stared at him as if they had found in his face a hidden secret; after a moment of meditation the mother said, "Will a man who sees and hears go out on a night that blinds the eyes and deafens the ears?" And the youth stated quietly, "I was expelled from the convent." "Expelled!" exclaimed Rachel; and Miriam repeated the same word in unison with her mother.

He lifted his head, regretting his words, for he was afraid lest their love and sympathy be converted into hatred and disrespect; but when he looked at them and found the rays of mercy still emanating from their eyes, and their bodies vibrating with anxiety to learn further, his voice choked and he continued, "Yes, I was expelled from the convent because I could not dig my grave with my own hands, and my heart grew weary of lying and pilfering. I was expelled from the convent because my soul refused to enjoy the bounty of a people who surrendered themselves to ignorance. I was driven away because I could not find rest in the comfortable rooms, built with the money of the poor fellahin. My stomach could not hold bread baked with the tears of orphans. My lips could not utter prayers sold for gold and food by the heads to the simple and faithful people. I was expelled from the convent like a filthy leper because I was repeating to the monks the rules that qualified them to their present position."

Silence prevailed while Rachel and Miriam were contemplating his words and gazing at him, when they asked, "Are your father and mother living?" And he responded, "I have no father or mother nor a place that is my home." Rachel drew a deep sigh and Miriam turned her face toward the wall to hide her merciful and loving tears.

As a withering flower is brought back to life by dew drops that dawn pours into its begging petals, so the youth's anxious heart was enlivened by his benefactors' affection and kindness. He looked at them as a soldier looks upon his liberators who rescue him from the grip of the enemy, and he resumed, "I lost my parents before I reached the age of seven. The village priest took me to Deir Kizhaya and left me at the disposal of the monks who were happy to take me in and put me in charge of the cows and sheep, which I led each day to the pasture. When I attained the age of fifteen, they put on me this black robe and led me into the altar whereupon the head priest addressed me saying, "Swear by the name of God and all saints, and make a vow to live a virtuous life of poverty and obedience." I repeated the words before I realized their significance or comprehended his own interpretation of poverty, virtue and obedience.

My name was Khalil, and since that time the monks addressed me as Brother Mobaarak,* but they never did treat me as a brother. They ate the most palatable foods and drank the finest wine, while I lived on dry vegetables and water, mixed

* Coincidentally, Mobaarak was the name of the Right Reverend Maronite Archbishop who officiated at Kahlil Gibran's last rites. (Editor's note.)

with tears. They slumbered in soft beds while I slept on a stone slab in a dark and cold room by the shed. Oftentimes I asked myself, "When will I become a monk and share with those fortunate priests their bounty? When will my heart stop craving for the food they eat and the wine they drink? When will I cease to tremble with fear before my superior?" But all my hopes were in vain, for I was kept in the same state; and in addition to caring for the cattle, I was obliged to move heavy stones on my shoulders and to dig pits and ditches. I sustained life on a few morsels of bread given to me in reward for my toil. I knew of no other place to which I might go, and the clergymen at the convent had caused me to abhor everything they were doing. They had poisoned my mind until I commenced to think that the whole world was an ocean of sorrows and miseries and that the convent was the only port of salvation. But when I discovered the source of their food and gold, I was happy that I did not share it."

Khalil straightened himself and looked about with wonder, as if he had found something beautiful standing before him in that wretched hut. Rachel and Miriam remained silent and he proceeded, "God, who took my father and exiled me as an orphan to the convent, did not want me to spend all my life walking blindly toward a dangerous jungle; nor did He wish me to be a miserable slave for the rest of my life. God opened my eyes and ears and showed me the bright light and made me hear Truth when Truth was talking."

Rachel thought aloud, "Is there any light, other than the sun, that shines over all the people? Are human beings capable of understanding the Truth?" Khalil returned, "The true light is that which emanates from within man, and reveals the secrets of the heart to the soul, making it happy and contented with life. Truth is like the stars; it does not appear except from behind obscurity of the night. Truth is like all beautiful things in the world; it does not disclose its desirability except to those who first feel the influence of falsehood. Truth is a deep kindness that teaches us to be content in our everyday life and share with the people the same happiness."

Rachel rejoined, "Many are those who live according to their goodness, and many are those who believe that compassion to others is the shadow of the law of God to man; but still, they do not rejoice in life, for they remain miserable until death." Khalil replied, "Vain are the beliefs and teachings that make man miserable, and false is the goodness that leads him into sorrow and despair, for it is man's purpose to be happy on this earth and lead the way to felicity and preach its gospel wherever he goes. He who does not see the kingdom of heaven in this life will never see it in the coming life. We came not into this life by exile, but we came as innocent creatures of God, to learn how to worship the holy and eternal spirit and seek the hidden secrets within ourselves from the beauty of life. This is the truth which I have learned from the teachings of the Nazarene. This is the light that came from within me and showed me the dark corners of the convent that threatened my life. This is the deep secret which the beautiful valleys and fields revealed to me when I was hungry, sitting lonely and weeping under the shadow of the trees.

This is the religion as the convent should impart it; as God wished it; as Jesus taught it. One day, as my soul became intoxicated with the heavenly intoxication of Truth's beauty, I stood bravely before the monks who were gathering in the garden, and criticized their wrong deeds saying, 'Why do you spend your days here and enjoy the bounty of the poor, whose bread you eat was made with the sweat of their bodies and the tears of their hearts? Why are you living in the shadow of parasitism, segregating yourselves from the people who are in need of knowledge? Why are you depriving the country of your help? Jesus has sent you as lambs amongst the wolves; what has made you as wolves amongst the lambs? Why are you fleeing from mankind and from God who created you? If you are better than the people who walk in the procession of life, you should go to them and better their lives; but if you think they are better than you, you should desire to learn from them. How do you take an oath and vow to live in poverty, then forget what you have said and live in luxury? How do you swear an obedience to God and then revolt against all that religion means? How do you adopt virtue as your rule when your heart is full of lusts? You pretend that you are killing your bodies, but in fact you are killing your souls. You feign to abhor the earthly things, but your heart is swollen with greed. You have the people believe in you as a religious teacher; truly speaking you are like busy cattle who divert themselves from knowledge by grazing in a green and beautiful pasture. Let us restore to the needy the vast land of the convent and give back to them the silver and gold we took from them. Let us disperse from our aloofness and serve the weak who made us strong, and cleanse the country in which we live. Let us teach this miserable nation to smile and rejoice with heaven's bounty and glory of life and freedom.

The people's tears are more beautiful and God-joined than the ease and tranquility to which you have accustomed yourselves in this place. The sympathy that touches the neighbour's heart is more supreme than the hidden virtue in the unseen corners of the convent. A word of compassion to the weak criminal or prostitute is nobler than the long prayer which we repeat emptily every day in the temple."

At this time Khalil took a deep breath. Then he lifted his eyes toward Rachel and Miriam saying, "I was saying all of these things to the monks and they were listening with an air of perplexity, as if they could not believe that a young man would dare stand before them and utter such bold words. When I finished, one of the monks approached and angrily said to me, 'How dare you talk in such fashion in our presence?' And another one came laughing and added, 'Did you learn all this from the cows and pigs you tended in the fields?' And a third one stood up and threatened me saying, 'You shall be punished, heretic!' Then they dispersed as though running away from a leper. Some of them complained to the head priest who summoned me before him at eventide. The monks took delight in anticipation of my suffering, and there was glee on their faces when I was ordered to be scourged and put into prison for forty days and nights. They led me into the dark cell where I spent the time lying in that grave without seeing the light. I could not tell the end of the night from the beginning of the day, and could feel nothing but crawling insects and the earth under me. I could hear naught save the tramping of the feet when my morsel of bread and dish of water mixed with vinegar were brought to me at great intervals.

When I came out of the prison I was weak and frail, and the monks believed that they had cured me of thinking, and that they had killed my soul's desire. They thought that hunger and thirst had choked the kindness which God placed in my heart. In my forty days of solitude I endeavoured to find a method by which I could help these monks to see the light and hear the true song of life, but all of my ponderings were in vain, for the thick veil which the long ages had woven around their eyes could not be torn away in a short time; and the mortar with which ignorance had cemented their ears was hardened and could not be removed by the touch of soft fingers."

68

Silence prevailed for a moment, and then Miriam looked at her mother as if asking her permission to let her talk. She said, "You must have talked to the monks again, if they selected this terrible night in which to banish you from the convent. They should learn to be kind even to their enemies."

Khalil returned, "This evening, as the thunder storms and warring elements raged in the sky, I withdrew myself from the monks who were crouching about the fire, telling tales and humorous stories. When they saw me alone they commenced to place their wit at my expense. I was reading my Gospel and contemplating the beautiful sayings of Jesus that made me forget for the time the enraged nature and belligerent elements of the sky, when they approached me with a new spirit of ridicule. I ignored them by occupying myself and looking through the window, but they became furious because my silence dried the laughter of their hearts and the taunting of their lips. One of them said, 'What are you reading, Great Reformer?' In response to his inquiry, I opened

69

my book and read aloud the following passage, 'But when he saw many of the Pharisees and Saducees come to his baptism, he said unto them, "O generation of vipers, who hath warned you to flee from the wrath to come? Bring forth therefore fruits for repentance; And think not to say within yourselves, 'We have Abraham to our father;' " for I say unto you, that God is able of these stones to raise children unto Abraham. And now also the axe is laid unto the root of the trees; therefore every tree which bringeth not forth good fruit is hewn down, and cast into the fire.'

As I read to them these words of John the Baptist, the monks became silent as if an invisible hand strangled their spirits, but they took false courage and commenced laughing. One of them said, 'We have read these words many times, and we are not in need of a cow grazier to repeat them to us.'

I protested, 'If you had read these words and comprehended their meaning, these poor villagers would not have frozen or starved to death.' When I said this, one of the monks slapped my face as if

I had spoken evil of the priests; another kicked me and a third took the book from me and a fourth one called the head priest who hurried to the scene shaking with anger. He cried out, 'Arrest this rebel and drag him from this sacred place, and let the storm's fury teach him obedience. Take him away and let nature do unto him the will of God, and then wash your hands of the poisonous germs of heresy infesting his raiment. If he should return pleading for forgiveness, do not open the door for him, for the viper will not become a dove if placed in a cage, nor will the briar bear figs if planted in the vineyards.'

In accordance with the command, I was dragged out by the laughing monks. Before they locked the door behind me, I heard one saying, 'Yesterday you were king of cows and pigs, and today you are dethroned, Oh Great Reformer; go now and be the king of wolves and teach them how to live in their lairs.'"

Khalil sighed deeply, then turned his face and looked toward the flaming fire. With a sweet and loving voice, and with a pained countenance he said, "Thus was I expelled from the convent, and thus did the monks deliver me over to the hands of Death. I fought through the night blindly; the heavy wind was tearing my robe and the piling snow was trapping my feet and pulling me down until I fell, crying desperately for help. I felt that no one heard me except Death, but a power which is all knowledge and mercy had heard my cry. That power did not want me to die before I had learned what is left of life's secrets. That power sent you both to me to save my life from the depth of the abyss and non-existence."

Rachel and Miriam felt as if their spirits understood the mystery of his soul, and they became his partners in feeling and understanding. Notwithstanding her will, Rachel stretched forth and gently touched his hand while tears coursed down from her eyes, and she said, "He who has been chosen by heaven as a defender of Truth will not perish by heaven's own storms and snow." And Miriam added, "The storms and snow may kill the flowers, but cannot deaden the seeds, for the snow keeps them warm from the killing frost."

Khalil's face brightened upon hearing those words of encouragement, and he said, "If you do not look upon me as a rebel and an heretic as the monks did, the persecution which I have sustained in the convent is the symbol of an oppressed nation that has not yet attained knowledge; and this night in which I was on the verge of death is like a revolution that precedes full justice. And from a sensitive woman's heart springs the happiness of mankind, and from the kindness of her noble spirit comes mankind's affection."

He closed his eyes and leaned down on the pillow; the two women did not bother him with further conversation for they knew that the weariness caused by long exposure had allured and captured his eyes. Khalil slept like a lost child who had finally found safety in his mother's arms.

Rachel and her daughter slowly walked to their bed and sat there watching him as if they had found in his trouble-torn face an attraction bringing their souls and hearts closer to him. And the mother whispered, saying, "There is a strange power in his closed eyes that speaks in silence and stimulates the soul's desires."

And Miriam rejoined, "His hands, Mother, are like those of Christ in the Church." The mother replied, "His face possesses at the same time a woman's tenderness and a man's boldness."

And the wings of slumber carried the women's spirits into the world of dream, and the fire went down and turned into ashes, while the light of the oil lamp dimmed gradually and disappeared. The fierce tempest continued its roar, and the obscured sky spread layers of snow, and the strong wind scattered them to the right and left.

IV

Five days passed, and the sky was still heavy with snow, burying the mountains and prairies relentlessly. Khalil made three attempts to resume his journey toward the plains, but Rachel restrained him each time, saying, "Do not give up your life to the blind elements, brother; remain here, for the bread that suffices two will also feed three, and the fire will still be burning after your departure as it was before your arrival. We are poor, brother, but like the rest of the people, we live our lives before the face of the sun and mankind, and God gives us our daily bread."

And Miriam was begging him with her kind glances, and pleading with her deep sighs, for since he entered the hut she felt the presence of a divine power in her soul sending forth life and light into her heart and awakening new affection in the Holy of Holies of her spirit. For the first time she experienced the feeling which made her heart like a white rose that sips the dew drops from the dawn and breathes its fragrance into the endless firmament.

There is no affection purer and more soothing to the spirit than the one hidden in the heart of a maiden who awakens suddenly and fills her own spirit with heavenly music that makes her days like poet's dreams and her nights prophetic. There is no secret in the mystery of life stronger and more beautiful than that attachment which converts the silence of a virgin's spirit into a perpetual awareness that makes a person forget the past, for it kindles fiercely in his heart the sweet and over-whelming hope of the coming future.

The Lebanese woman distinguishes herself from the woman of other nations by her simplicity. The manner in which she is trained restricts her prog-ress educationally, and stands as a hindrance to her future. Yet for this reason, she finds herself in-quiring of herself as to the inclination and mys-tery of her heart. The Lebanese young woman is like a spring that comes out from the heart of the earth and follows its course through winding de-pressions, but since it cannot find an outlet to the sea, it turns into a calm lake that reflects upon its growing surface the glittering stars and the shining moon. Khalil felt the vibration of Miriam's heart twining steadily about his soul, and he knew that the divine torch that illuminated his heart had also touched her heart. He rejoiced for the first time, like a parched brook greeting the rain, but he blamed himself for his haste, believing that this spiritual understanding would pass like a cloud when he departed from that village. He often spoke to himself saying, "What is this mystery that plays so great a part in our lives? What is this Law that drives us into a rough road and stops us just before we reach the face of the sun where we might rejoice? What is this power that elevates our spirits until we reach the mountain top, smiling and glorying, then suddenly we are cast to the depths of the valley, weeping and suffering? What is this life that embraces us like a lover one day, and fights us like an enemy the second day? Was I not persecuted yesterday? Did I not survive hunger and thirst and suffering and mockery for the sake of the Truth which heaven had awakened in my heart? Did I not tell the monks that happiness through Truth is the will and the purpose of God in man? Then what is this fear? And why do I close my eyes to the light that emanates from that young woman's eyes? I am expelled and she is poor, but is it on bread only that man can live? Are we not, between famine and plenty, like trees between winter and summer? But what would Rachel say if she knew that my heart and her daughter's heart came to an understanding in silence, and approached close to each other and neared the circle of the Supreme Light? What would she say if she discovered that the young man whose life she saved longed to gaze upon her daughter? What would the simple villagers say if they knew that a young man, reared in the convent, came to their village by necessity and expulsion, and desired to live near a beautiful maiden? Will they listen to me if I tell them that he who leaves the convent to live amongst them is like a bird that flies from the bruising walls of the cage to the light of freedom? What will Sheik Abbas say if he hears my story? What will the priest of the village do if he learns of the cause for my expulsion?"

Khalil was talking to himself in this fashion while sitting by the fireplace, meditating the flames, symbol of his love; and Miriam was stealing a glance now and then at his face and reading his dreams through his eyes, and hearing the echo of his thoughts, and feeling the touch of his love, even though no word was uttered.

One night, as he stood by the small transom that

faced the valleys where the trees and rocks were shrouded with white coverings, Miriam came and stood by him, looking at the sky. As their eyes turned and met, he drew a deep sigh and shut his eyes as if his soul were sailing in the spacious sky looking for a word. He found no word necessary, for the silence spoke for them. Miriam ventured, "Where will you go when the snow meets the stream and the paths are dry?" His eyes opened, looking beyond the horizon, and he explained, "I shall follow the path to wherever my destiny and my mission for Truth shall take me." Miriam sighed sadly and offered, "Why will you not remain here and live close to us? Is it that you are obliged to go elsewhere?" He was moved by her kindness and sweet words, but protested, "The villagers here will not accept an expelled monk as their neighbour, and will not permit him to breathe the air they breathe because they believe that the enemy of the convent is an infidel, cursed by God and his saints." Miriam resorted to silence, for the Truth that pained her prevented further talk. Then Khalil turned aside and explained,

"Miriam, these villagers are taught by those in authority to hate everyone who thinks freely; they are trained to remain afar from those whose minds soar aloft; God does not like to be worshipped by an ignorant man who imitates someone else; if I remained in this village and asked the people to worship as they please, they would say that I am an infidel disobeying the authority that was given to the priest by God. If I asked them to listen and hear the voices of their hearts and do according to the will of the spirit within, they would say that I am an evil man who wants them to do away with the clergy that God placed between heaven and earth." Khalil looked straight into Miriam's eyes, and with a voice that bespoke the sound of silver strings said, "But, Miriam, there is a magic power in this village that possesses me and engulfs my soul; a power so divine that it causes me to forget my pain. In this village I met Death to his very face, and in this place my soul embraced God's spirit. In this village there is a beautiful flower grown over the lifeless grass; its beauty attracts my heart and its fragrance fills its domain. Shall I leave this important flower and go out preaching the ideas that caused my expulsion from the convent, or shall I remain by the side of that flower and dig a grave and bury my thoughts and truths among its neighboring thorns? What shall I do, Miriam?" Upon hearing these words, she shivered like a lily before the frolicsome breeze of the dawn. Her heart glowed through her eyes when she faltered, "We are both in the hands of a mysterious and merciful power. Let it do its will."

At that moment the two hearts joined and thereafter both spirits were one burning torch illuminating their lives.

V

Since the beginning of the creation and up to our present time, certain clans, rich by inheritance, in co-operation with the clergy, had appointed themselves the administrators of the people. It is an old, gaping wound in the heart of society that cannot be removed except by intense removal of ignorance.

The man who acquires his wealth by inheritance builds his mansion with the weak poor's money. The clergyman erects his temple upon the graves and bones of the devoted worshippers. The prince grasps the fellah's arms while the priest empties his pocket; the ruler looks upon the sons of the fields with frowning face, and the bishop consoles them with his smile, and between the frown of the tiger and the smile of the wolf the flock is perished; the ruler claims himself as king of the law, and the priest as the representative of God, and between these two, the bodies are destroyed and the souls wither into nothing.

In Lebanon, that mountain rich in sunlight and poor in knowledge, the noble and the priest joined hands to exploit the farmer who ploughed the land and reaped the crop in order to protect himself from the sword of the ruler and the curse of the priest. The rich man in Lebanon stood proudly by his palace and shouted at the multitudes saying, "The Sultan has appointed me as your lord." And the priest stands before the altar saying, "God has delegated me as an executive of your souls." But the Lebanese resorted to silence, for the dead could not talk.

Sheik Abbas had friendship in his heart for the clergymen, because they were his allies in choking the people's knowledge and reviving the spirit of stern obedience among his workers.

That evening, when Khalil and Miriam were approaching the throne of Love, and Rachel was looking upon them with the eyes of affection, Father Elias informed Sheik Abbas that the head priest had expelled a rebellious young man from the convent and that he had taken refuge at the house of Rachel, the widow of Samaan Ramy. And the priest was not satisfied with the little information he gave the Sheik, but commented, "The demon they chased out of the convent cannot become an angel in this village, and the fig tree which is hewn and cast into the fire, does not bear fruit while burning. If we wish to clean this village of the filth of this beast, we must drive him away as the monks did." And the Sheik inquired, "Are you certain that the young man will be a bad influence upon our people? Is it not better for us to keep him and make him a worker in our vineyards? We are in need of strong men."

The priest's face showed his disagreement. Combing his beard with his fingers, he said shrewdly, "If he were fit to work, he would not have been expelled from the convent. A student who works in the convent, and who happened to spend last night at my house, informed me that this young man had violated the rules of the head priest by preaching danger-ridden ideas among the monks, and he quoted him as saying, "Restore the fields and the vineyards and the silver of the convent to the poor and scatter it in all directions; and help the people who are in need of knowledge; by thus doing, you will please your Father in Heaven."

On hearing these words, Sheik Abbas leaped to his feet, and like a tiger making ready to strike the victim, he walked to the door and called to the servants, ordering them to report immediately. Three men entered, and the Sheik commanded, "In the house of Rachel, the widow of Samaan Ramy, there is a young man wearing a monk's raiment. Tie him and bring him here. If that woman objects to his arrest, drag her out by her braided hair over the snow and bring her with him, for he who helps evil is evil himself." The men bowed obediently and hurried to Rachel's home while the priest and the Sheik discussed the type of punishment to be awarded to Khalil and Rachel.

VI

The day was over and the night had come spreading its shadow over those wretched huts, heavily laden with snow. The stars finally appeared in the sky, like hopes in the coming eternity after the suffering of death's agony. The doors and windows were closed and the lamps were lighted. The fellahin sat by the fireside warming their bodies. Rachel, Miriam and Khalil were seated at a rough wooden table eating their evening meal when there was a knock at the door and three men entered. Rachel and Miriam were frightened, but Khalil remained calm, as if he

85

awaited the coming of those men. One of the Sheik's servants walked toward Khalil, laid his hand upon his shoulder and asked, "Are you the one who was expelled from the convent?" And Khalil responded, "Yes, I am the one, what do you want?" The man replied, "We are ordered to arrest you and take you with us to Sheik Abbas' home, and if you object we shall drag you out like a butchered sheep over the snow."

Rachel turned pale as she exclaimed, "What crime has he committed, and why do you want to tie him and drag him out?" The two women pleaded with tearful voices, saying, "He is one individual in the hands of three and it is cowardly of you to make him suffer." The men became enraged and shouted, "Is there any woman in this village who opposes the Sheik's order?" And he drew forth a rope and started to tie Khalil's hands. Khalil lifted his head proudly, and a sorrowful smile appeared on his lips when he said, "I feel sorry for you men, because you are a strong and blind instrument in the hands of a man who oppresses the weak with the strength of your arms.

You are slaves of ignorance. Yesterday I was a man like you, but tomorrow you shall be free in mind as I am now. Between us there is a deep precipice that chokes my calling voice and hides my reality from you, and you cannot hear or see. Here I am, tie my hands and do as you please." The three men were moved by his talk and it seemed that his voice had awakened in them a new spirit, but the voice of Sheik Abbas still rang in their minds, warning them to complete the mission. They bound his hands and led him out silently with a heavy conscience. Rachel and Miriam followed them to the Sheik's home, like the daughters of Jerusalem who followed Christ to Mount Calvary.

VII

Regardless of its import, news travels swiftly among the fellahin in the small villages, because their absence from the realm of society makes them anxious and busy in discussing the happenings of their limited environs. In winter, when the fields are slumbering under the quilts of snow, and when human life is taking refuge and warming itself by the fireside, the villagers become most inclined to learn of current news in order to occupy themselves.

It was not long after Khalil was arrested, when the story spread like a contagious disease amongst the villagers. They left their huts and hurried like an army from every direction into the home of Sheik Abbas. When Khalil's feet stepped in the Sheik's home, the residence was crowded with men, women and children who were endeavouring for a glance at the infidel who was expelled from the convent. They were also anxious to see Rachel and her daughter, who had helped Khalil in spreading the hellish disease of heresy in the pure sky of their village.

The Sheik took the seat of judgment and beside him sat Father Elias, while the throng was gazing at the pinioned youth who stood bravely before them. Rachel and Miriam were standing behind Khalil and trembling with fear. But what could fear do to the heart of a woman who found Truth and followed him? What could the scorn of the crowd do to the soul of a maiden who had been awakened by Love? Sheik Abbas looked at the young man, and with a thundering voice he interrogated him saying, "What is your name, man?" "Khalil is my name," answered the youth. The Sheik returned, "Who are your father and mother and relatives, and where were you born?" Khalil turned toward the fellahin, who looked upon him with hateful eyes, and said, "The oppressed poor are my clan and my relatives, and this vast country is my birthplace."

Sheik Abbas, with an air of ridicule, said, "Those people whom you claim as kin demand that you be punished, and the country you assert as your birthplace objects to your being a member of its people." Khalil replied, "The ignorant nations arrest their good men and turn them into their despots; and a country, ruled by a tyrant, persecutes those who try to free the people from the yoke of slavery. But will a good son leave his mother if she is ill? Will a merciful man deny his brother who is miserable? Those poor men who arrested me and brought me here today are the same ones who surrendered their lives to you yesterday. And this vast earth that disapproves my existence is the one that does not yawn and swallow the greedy despots."

The Sheik uttered a loud laugh, as if wanting to depress the young man's spirit and prevent him from influencing the audience. He turned to Khalil and said impressively, "You cattle grazier, do you think that we will show more mercy than did the monks, who expelled you from the convent? Do you think that we feel pity for a dangerous agitator?" Khalil responded, "It is true that I was a cattle grazier, but I am glad that I was not a butcher. I led my herds to the rich pastures and never grazed them on arid land. I led my animals to pure springs and kept them from contaminated marshes. At eventide I brought them safely to their shed and never left them in the valleys as prey for the wolves. Thus I have treated the animals; and if you had pursued my course and treated human beings as I treated my flock, these poor people would not live in wretched huts and suffer the pangs of poverty, while you are living like Nero in this gorgeous mansion."

The Sheik's forehead glittered with drops of perspiration, and his smirk turned into anger, but he tried to show only calm by pretending that he did not heed Khalil's talk, and he expostulated, pointing at Khalil with his finger, "You are a heretic, and we shall not listen to your ridiculous talk; we summoned you to be tried as a criminal, and you realize that you are in the presence of the Lord of this village who is empowered to represent his Excellency Emir Ameen Shebab. You are standing before Father Elias, the representative of the Holy Church whose teachings you have opposed. Now, defend yourself, or kneel down before these people and we will pardon you and make you a cattle grazier, as you were in the convent." Khalil calmly returned, "A criminal is not to be tried by another criminal, as an atheist will not defend himself before sinners." And Khalil looked at the audience and spoke to them saying, "My brethren, the man whom you call the Lord of your fields, and to whom you have yielded thus long, has brought me to be tried before you in this edifice which he built upon the graves of your forefathers. And the man who became a pastor of your church through your faith, has come to judge me and help you to humiliate me and increase my sufferings. You have hurried to this place from every direction to see me suffer and hear me plead for mercy. You have left your huts in order to witness your pinioned son and brother. You have come to see the prey trembling between the paws of a ferocious beast. You came here tonight to view an infidel standing before the judges. I am the criminal and I am the heretic who has been expelled from the convent. The tempest brought me into your village. Listen to my protest, and do not be merciful, but be just, for mercy is bestowed upon the guilty criminal, while justice is all that an innocent man requires.

I select you now as my jury, because the will of the people is the will of God. Awaken your hearts and listen carefully and then prosecute me according to the dictates of your conscience. You have been told that I am an infidel, but you have not been informed of what crime or sin I have committed. You have seen me tied like a thief, but you have not yet heard about my offenses, for wrongdoings are not revealed in this court, while punishment comes out like thunder. My crime, dear fellowmen, is my understanding of your plight, for I felt the weight of the irons which have been placed upon your necks. My sin is my heartfelt sorrows for your women; it is my sympathy for your children who suck life from your breast mixed with the shadow of death. I am one of you, and my forefathers lived in these valleys and died under the same yoke which is bending your heads now. I believe in God who listens to the call of your suffering souls, and I believe in the Book that makes all of us brothers before the face of heaven. I believe in the teachings that make us all equal, and that render us unpinioned upon this earth, the stepping place of the careful feet of God.

As I was grazing my cows at the convent, and contemplating the sorrowful condition you tolerate, I heard a desperate cry coming from your miserable homes—a cry of oppressed souls—a cry of broken hearts which are locked in your bodies as slaves to the lord of these fields. As I looked, I found me in the convent and you in the fields, and I saw you as a flock of lambs following a wolf to the lair; and as I stopped in the middle of the road to aid the lambs, I cried for help and the wolf snapped me with his sharp teeth.

I have sustained imprisonment, thirst, and hunger for the sake of Truth that hurts only the body. I have undergone suffering beyond endurance because I turned your sad sighs into a crying voice that rang and echoed in every corner of the convent. I never felt fear, and my heart never tired, for your painful cry was injecting a new strength into me every day, and my heart was healthy. You may ask yourself now saying, 'When did we ever cry for help, and who dares open his lips?' But I say unto you, your souls are crying every day, and pleading for help every night, but you cannot hear them, for the dying man cannot hear his own heart rattling, while those who are standing by his bedside can surely hear. The slaughtered bird, in spite of his will, dances painfully and unknowingly, but those who witness the dance know what caused it. In what hour of the day do you sigh painfully? Is it in the morning, when love of existence cries at you and tears the veil of slumber off your eyes and leads you like slaves into the fields? Is it at noon, when you wish to sit under a tree to protect yourself from the burning sun? Or at eventide, when you return home hungry, wishing for sustaining food instead of a meagre morsel and impure water? Or at night when fatigue throws you upon your rough bed, and as soon as slumber closes your eyes, you sit up with open eyes, fearing that the Sheik's voice is ringing in your ears?

In what season of the year do you not lament yourselves? Is it in Spring, when nature puts on her beautiful dress and you go out to meet her with tattered raiment? Or in Summer, when you harvest the wheat and gather the sheaves of corn and fill the shelves of your master with the crop, and when the reckoning comes you receive naught but hay and tare? Is it in Autumn, when you pick the fruits and carry the grapes into the wine-press, and in reward for your toil you receive a jar of vinegar and a bushel of acorns? Or in Winter, when you are confined to your huts laden with snow, do you sit by the fire and tremble when the enraged sky urges you to escape from your weak minds?

This is the life of the poor; this is the perpetual cry I hear. This is what makes my spirit revolt against the oppressors and despise their conduct. When I asked the monks to have mercy upon you, they thought that I was an atheist, and expulsion was my lot. Today I came here to share this miserable life with you, and to mix my tears with yours. Here I am now, in the grip of your worst enemy. Do you realize that this land you are working like slaves was taken from your fathers when the law was written on the sharp edge of the sword? The monks deceived your ancestors and took all their fields and vineyards when the religious rules were written on the lips of the priests. Which man or woman is not influenced by the lord of the fields to do according to the will of the priests? God said,

'With the sweat of thy brow, thou shall eat thy bread.' But Sheik Abbas is eating his bread baked in the years of your lives and drinking his wine mixed with your tears. Did God distinguish this man from the rest of you while in his mother's womb? Or is it your sin that made you his property? Jesus said, 'Gratis you have taken and gratis you shall give. . . . Do not possess gold, nor silver, neither copper.' Then what teachings allow the clergymen to sell their prayers for pieces of gold and silver? In the silence of the night you pray saying, 'Give us today our daily bread.' God has given you this land from which to draw your daily bread, but what authority has He given the monks to take this land and this bread away from you?

You curse Judas because he sold his Master for a few pieces of silver, but you bless those who sell Him every day. Judas repented and hanged himself for his wrongdoing, but these priests walk proudly, dressed with beautiful robes, resplendent with shining crosses hanging over their chests. You teach your children to love Christ and at the same time you instruct them to obey those who oppose His teachings and violate His law.

The apostles of Christ were stoned to death in order to revive in you the Holy Spirit, but the monks and the priests are killing that spirit in you so they may live on your pitiful bounty. What persuades you to live such a life in this universe, full of misery and oppression? What prompts you to kneel before that horrible idol which has been erected upon the bones of your fathers? What treasure are you reserving for your posterity?

Your souls are in the grip of the priests, and your bodies are in the closing jaws of the rulers. What thing in life can you point at and say 'this is mine!' My fellowmen, do you know the priest you fear? He is a traitor who uses the Gospel as a threat to ransom your money . . . a hypocrite wearing a cross and using it as a sword to cut your veins . . . a wolf disguised in lambskin . . . a glutton who respects the tables more than the altars . . . a gold-hungry creature who follows the Denar to the farthest land . . . a cheat pilfering from widows and orphans. He is a queer being, with an eagle's beak, a tiger's clutches, a hyena's teeth and a viper's clothes. Take the Book away from him and tear his raiment off and pluck his beard and do whatever you wish unto him; then place in his hand one Denar, and he will forgive you smilingly.

Slap his face and spit on him and step on his neck; then invite him to sit at your board. He will immediately forget and untie his belt and gladly fill his stomach with your food.

Curse him and ridicule him; then send him a jar of wine or a basket of fruit. He will forgive you your sins. When he sees a woman, he turns his face, saying, 'Go from me, Oh, daughter of Babylon.' Then he whispers to himself saying, 'Marriage is better than coveting.' He sees the young men and women walking in the procession of Love, and he lifts his eyes toward heaven and says, 'Vanity of vanities, all is vanity.' And in his solitude he talks to himself saying, 'May the laws and traditions that deny me the joys of life, be abolished.'

He preaches to the people saying, 'Judge not,

99

lest ye be judged.' But he judges all those who abhor his deeds and sends them to hell before Death separates them from this life.

When he talks he lifts his head toward heaven, but at the same time, his thoughts are crawling like snakes through your pockets.

He addresses you as beloved children, but his heart is empty of paternal love, and his lips never smile at a child, nor does he carry an infant between his arms.

He tells you, while shaking his head, 'Let us keep away from earthly things, for life passes like a cloud.' But if you look thoroughly at him, you will find that he is gripping on to life, lamenting the passing of yesterday, condemning the speed of today, and waiting fearfully for tomorrow.

He asks you for charity when he has plenty to give; if you grant his request, he will bless you publicly, and if you refuse him, he will curse you secretly.

In the temple he asks you to help the needy, and about his house the needy are begging for bread, but he cannot see or hear.

He sells his prayers, and he who does not buy is an infidel, excommunicated from Paradise.

This is the creature of whom you are afraid. This is the monk who sucks your blood. This is the priest who makes the sign of the Cross with the right hand, and clutches your throat with the left hand.

This is the pastor whom you appoint as your servant, but he appoints himself as your master.

This is the shadow that embraces your souls from birth until death.

This is the man who came to judge me tonight because my spirit revolted against the enemies of Jesus the Nazarene Who loved all and called us brothers, and Who died on the Cross for us."

Khalil felt that there was understanding in the villagers' hearts; his voice brightened and he resumed his discourse saying, "Brethren, you know that Sheik Abbas has been appointed as Master of this village by Emir Shehab, the Sultan's representative and Governor of the Province, but I ask you if anyone has seen that power appoint the Sultan as the god of this country. That Power, my fellowmen, cannot be seen, nor can you hear it talk, but you can feel its existence in the depths of your hearts. It is that Power which you worship and pray for every day saying, 'Our Father which art in heaven.' Yes, your Father Who is in heaven is the one Who appoints kings and princes, for He is powerful and above all. But do you think that your Father, Who loved you and showed you the right path through His prophets, desires for you to be oppressed? Do you believe that God, Who brings forth the rain from heaven, and the wheat from the hidden seeds in the heart of the earth, desires for you to be hungry in order that but one man will enjoy His bounty? Do you believe that the Eternal Spirit Who reveals to you the wife's love, the children's pity and the neighbor's mercy, would have upon you a tyrant to enslave you through your life? Do you believe that the Eternal Law that made life beautiful, would send you a man to deny you of that happiness and lead you into the dark dungeon of painful Death? Do you believe that your physical strength, provided you by nature, belongs beyond your body to the rich?

You cannot believe in all these things, because if you do you will be denying the justice of God who made us all equal, and the light of Truth that shines upon all the peoples of the earth. What makes you struggle against yourselves, heart against body, and help those who enslave you while God has created you free on this earth?

Are you doing yourselves justice when you lift your eyes towards Almighty God and call him Father, and then turn around, bow your heads before a man, and call him Master?

Are you contented, as sons of God, with being slaves of man? Did not Christ call you brethren? Yet Sheik Abbas calls you servants. Did not Jesus make you free in Truth and Spirit? Yet the Emir made you slaves of shame and corruption. Did not Christ exalt you to heaven? Then why are you descending to hell? Did He not enlighten your hearts? Then why are you hiding your souls in darkness? God has placed a glowing torch in your hearts that glows in knowledge and beauty, and seeks the secrets of the days and nights; it is a sin to extinguish that torch and bury it in ashes. God

103

has created your spirits with wings to fly in the spacious firmament of Love and Freedom; it is pitiful that you cut your wings with your own hands and suffer your spirits to crawl like insects upon the earth."

Sheik Abbas observed in dismay the attentiveness of the villagers, and attempted to interrupt, but Khalil, inspired, continued, "God has sown in your hearts the seeds of Happiness; it is a crime that you dig those seeds out and throw them wilfully on the rocks so the wind will scatter them and the birds will pick them. God has given you children to rear, to teach them the truth and fill their hearts with the most precious things of existence. He wants you to bequeath upon them the joy of Life and the bounty of Life; why are they now strangers to their place of birth and cold creatures before the face of the Sun? A father who makes his son a slave is the father who gives his child a stone when he asks for bread. Have you not seen the birds of the sky training their young ones to fly? Why, then, do you teach your children to drag the shackles of slavery? Have you not seen the flowers of the valleys deposit their seeds in the sun-heated earth? Then why do you commit your children to the cold darkness?"

Silence prevailed for a moment, and it seemed as if Khalil's mind were crowded with pain. But now with a low and compelling voice he continued, "The words which I utter tonight are the same expressions that caused my expulsion from the convent. If the lord of your fields and the pastor of your church were to prey upon me and kill me tonight, I will die happy and in peace because I have fulfilled my mission and revealed to you the Truth which demons consider a crime. I have now completed the will of Almighty God."

There had been a magic message in Khalil's voice that forced the villagers' interest. The women were moved by the sweetness of his words and looked upon him as a messenger of peace, and their eyes were rich with tears.

Sheik Abbas and Father Elias were shaking with anger. As Khalil finished, he walked a few steps and stopped near Rachel and Miriam. Silence dominated the courtroom, and it seemed as if

Khalil's spirit hovered in that vast hall and diverted the souls of the multitude from fearing Sheik Abbas and Father Elias, who sat trembling in annoyance and guilt.

The Sheik stood suddenly and his face was pale. He looked toward the men who were standing about him as he said, "What has become of you, dogs? Have your hearts been poisoned? Has your blood stopped running and weakened you so that you cannot leap upon this criminal and cut him to pieces? What awful thing has he done to you?" Having finished reprimanding the men, he raised a sword and started toward the fettered youth, whereupon a strong villager walked to him, gripped his hand and said, "Lay down your weapon, Master, for he who draws the sword to kill, shall, by the sword, be killed!"

The Sheik trembled visibly and the sword fell from his hand. He addressed the man saying, "Will a weak servant oppose his Master and benefactor?" And the man responded, "The faithful servant does not share his Master in the committing of crimes; this young man has spoken naught but the truth." Another man stepped forward and assured, "This man is innocent and is worthy of honor and respect." And a woman raised her voice saying, "He did not swear at God or curse any saint; why do you call him heretic?" And Rachel asked, "What is his crime?" The Sheik shouted, "You are rebellious, you miserable widow; have you forgotten the fate of your husband who turned rebel six years ago?" Upon hearing these impulsive words, Rachel shivered with painful anger, for she had found the murderer of her husband. She choked her tears and looked upon the throng and cried out, "Here is the criminal you have been trying for six years to find; you hear him now confessing his guilt. He is the killer who has been hiding his crime. Look at him and read his face; study him well and observe his fright; he shivers like the last leaf on winter's tree. God has shown you that the Master whom you have always feared is a murderous criminal. He caused me to be a widow amongst these women, and my daughter an orphan amidst these children." Rachel's utterance fell like thunder upon the

107

Sheik's head, and the uproar of men and exaltation of women fell like firebrands upon him.

The priest assisted the Sheik to his seat. Then he called the servants and ordered them saying, "Arrest this woman who has falsely accused your Master of killing her husband; drag her and this young man into a dark prison, and any who oppose you will be criminals, excommunicated as he was from the Holy Church." The servants gave no heed to his command, but remained motionless staring at Khalil who was still bound with rope. Rachel stood at his right and Miriam at his left like a pair of wings ready to soar aloft into the spacious sky of Freedom.

His beard shaking with anger, Father Elias said, "Are you denying your Master for the sake of an infidel criminal and a shameless adulteress?" And the oldest one of the servants answered him saying, "We have served Sheik Abbas long for bread and shelter, but we have never been his slaves." Having thus spoken, the servant took off his cloak and turban and threw them before the Sheik and added, "I shall no longer require this raiment, nor do I wish my soul to suffer in the narrow house of a criminal." And all the servants did likewise and joined the crowd whose faces radiated with joy, symbol of Freedom and Truth. Father Elias finally saw that his authority had declined, and he left the place cursing the hour that brought Khalil to the village. A strong man strode to Khalil and untied his hands, looked at Sheik Abbas who fell like a corpse upon his seat, and boldly addressed him saying, "This fettered youth, whom you have brought here tonight to be tried as a criminal, has lifted our depressed spirits and enlightened our hearts with Truth and Knowledge. And this poor widow whom Father Elias referred to as a false accuser has revealed to us the crime you committed six years past. We came here tonight to witness the trial of an innocent youth and a noble soul. Now, heaven has opened our eyes and has shown us your atrocity; we shall leave you and ignore you and allow heaven to do its will."

Many voices were raised in that hall, and one could hear a certain man saying, "Let us leave this ill-famed residence for our homes." And another one remarking, "Let us follow this young man to Rachel's home and listen to his wise sayings and consoling wisdom." And a third one saying, "Let us seek his advice, for he knows our needs." And a fourth one calling out, "If we are seeking justice, let us complain to the Emir and tell him of Abbas' crime." And many were saying, "Let us petition the Emir to appoint Khalil as our Master and ruler, and tell the Bishop that Father Elias was a partner in these crimes." While the voices were rising and falling upon the Sheik's ears like sharp arrows, Khalil lifted his hands and calmed the villagers saying, "My brethren, do not seek haste, but rather listen and meditate. I ask you, in the name of my love and friendship for you, not to go to the Emir, for you will not find justice. Remember that a ferocious beast does not snap another one like him, neither should you go to the Bishop, for he knows well that the house cloven amid itself shall be ruined. Do not ask the Emir to appoint me as the Sheik in this village, for the faithful servant does not like to be an aid to the evil Master. If I deserve your kindness and love, let me live amongst you and share with you the happiness and sorrows of Life. Let me join hands and work with you at home and in the fields, for if I could not make myself one of you, I would be a hypocrite who does not live according to his sermon. And now, as the axe is laid unto the root of the tree, let us leave Sheik Abbas alone in the courtroom of his conscience and before the Supreme Court of God whose sun shines upon the innocent and the criminal."

Having thus spoken, he left the place, and the multitude followed him as if there were a divine power in him that attracted their hearts. The Sheik remained alone with the terrible silence, like a destroyed tower, suffering his defeat quietly, like a surrendering commander. When the multitude reached the church yard and the moon was just showing from behind the cloud, Khalil looked at them with the eyes of love like a good shepherd watching over his herd. He was moved with sympathy upon those villagers who symbolized an oppressed nation; and he stood like a prophet who saw all the nations of the East walking in those valleys and dragging empty souls and heavy hearts.

He raised both hands toward heaven and said, "From the bottom of these depths we call thee, Oh, Liberty. Give heed to us! From behind the darkness we raise our hands to thee, Oh, Liberty. Look upon us! Upon the snow, we worship before thee, Oh, Liberty. Have mercy on us! Before thy great throne we stand, hanging on our bodies the blood-stained garments of our forefathers, covering our heads with the dust of the graves mixed with their remains, carrying the swords that stabbed their hearts, lifting the spears that pierced their bodies, dragging the chains that slowed their feet, uttering the cry that wounded their throats, lamenting and repeating the song of our failure that echoed throughout the prison, and repeating the prayers that came from the depths of our fathers' hearts. Listen to us, Oh Liberty, and hear us. From the Nile to the Euphrates comes the wailing of the suffering souls, in unison with the cry of the abyss; and from the end of the East to the mountains of Lebanon, hands are stretched to you, trembling with the presence of Death. From the shores of the sea to the end of the Desert, tear-flooded eyes look beseechingly toward you. Come, Oh, Liberty, and save us.

In the wretched huts standing in the shadow of poverty and oppression, they beat at their bosoms, soliciting thy mercy; watch us, oh Liberty, and have mercy on us. In the pathways and in the houses miserable youth calls thee; in the churches and the mosques, the forgotten Book turns to thee; in the courts and in the palaces the neglected Law appeals to thee. Have mercy on us, Oh Liberty, and save us. In our narrow streets the merchant sells his days in order to make tribute to the exploiting thieves of the West, and none would give him advice. In the barren fields the fellah tills the soil and sows the seeds of his heart and nourishes them with his tears, but he reaps naught except thorns, and none would teach him the true path. In our arid plains the Bedouin roams barefoot and hungry, but none would have mercy on him; speak, Oh Liberty, and teach us! Our sick lambs are grazing upon the grassless prairie, our calves are gnawing on the roots of the trees, and our horses are feeding on dry plants. Come, Oh Liberty, and help us. We have been living in darkness since the beginning, and like prisoners they take us from one prison to another, while time ridicules our plight. When will dawn come? Until when shall we bear the scorn of the ages? Many a stone have we been dragging, and many a yoke has been placed upon our necks. Until when shall we bear this human outrage? The Egyptian slavery, the Babylonian exile, the tyranny of Persia, the despotism of the Romans, and the greed of Europe . . . all these things we have suffered. Where are we going now, and when shall we reach the sublime end of the rough roadway? From the clutches of Pharaoh to the paws of Nebuchadnezzar, to the iron hands of Alexander, to the swords of Herod, to the talons of Nero, and the sharp teeth of Demon . . . into whose hands are we now to fall, and when will Death come and take us, so we may rest at last?

With the strength of our arms we lifted the columns of the temple, and upon our backs we carried the mortar to build the great walls and the impregnable pyramids for the sake of glory. Until when shall we continue building such magnificent palaces and living in wretched huts? Until when shall we continue filling the bins of the rich with provisions, while sustaining weak life on dry morsels? Until when shall we continue weaving silk and wool for our lords and masters while we wear naught except tattered swaddles?

Through their wickedness we were divided amongst ourselves; and the better to keep their thrones and be at ease, they armed the Druze to fight the Arab, and stirred up the Shiite to attack the Sunnite, and encouraged the Kurdish to butcher the Bedouin, and cheered the Mohammedan to dispute with the Christian. Until when shall a brother continue killing his own brother upon his mother's bosom? Until when shall the Cross be kept apart from the Crescent * before the eyes of God? Oh Liberty, hear us, and speak in behalf of but one individual, for a great fire is

* The crescent is the emblem of the Mohammedan flag, flown over Syria during the Turkish rule. [Editor's note.]

started with a small spark. Oh Liberty, awaken
but one heart with the rustling of thy wings, for
from one cloud alone comes the lightning which
illuminates the pits of the valleys and the tops of
the mountains. Disperse with thy power these
black clouds and descend like thunder and destroy
the thrones that were built upon the bones and
skulls of our ancestors."

"Hear us, Oh Liberty;
Bring mercy, Oh Daughter of Athens;
Rescue us, Oh Sister of Rome;
Advise us, Oh Companion of Moses;
Help us, Oh Beloved of Mohammed;
Teach us, Oh Bride of Jesus;
Strengthen our hearts so we may live,
Or harden our enemies so we may perish
And live in peace eternally."

As Khalil was pouring forth his sentiment before heaven, the villagers were gazing at him in
reverence, and their love was springing forth in
unison with the song of his voice until they felt

that he became part of their hearts. After a short silence, Khalil brought his eyes upon the multitude and quietly said, "Night has brought us to the house of Sheik Abbas in order to realize the daylight; oppression has arrested us before the cold Space, so we may understand one another and gather like chicks under the wings of the Eternal Spirit. Now let us go to our homes and sleep until we meet again tomorrow."

Having thus spoken, he walked away, following Rachel and Miriam to their poor hovel. The throng departed and each went to his home, contemplating what he had seen and heard that memorable night. They felt that a burning torch of a new spirit had scoured their inner selves and led them into the right path. In an hour all the lamps were extinguished and Silence engulfed the whole village while Slumber carried the fellahin's souls into the world of strong dreams; but Sheik Abbas found no sleep all night, as he watched the phantoms of darkness and the horrible ghosts of his crimes in procession.

VIII

Two months had already passed and Khalil was still preaching and pouring his sentiments in the villagers' hearts, reminding them of their usurped rights and showing them the greed and oppression of the rulers and the monks. They listened to him with care, for he was a source of pleasure; his words fell upon their hearts like rain upon thirsty land. In their solitude, they repeated Khalil's sayings as they did their daily prayers. Father Elias commenced fawning upon them to regain their friendship; he became docile since the villagers found out that he was the Sheik's ally in crime, and the fellahin ignored him.

Sheik Abbas had a nervous suffering, and walked through his mansion like a caged tiger. He issued commands to his servants, but no one answered except the echo of his voice inside the marble walls. He shouted at his men, but no one came to his aid except his poor wife who suffered the pang of his cruelty as much as the villagers did. When Lent came and Heaven announced the coming of Spring, the days of the Sheik expired with the passing of Winter. He died after a long agony, and his soul was carried away on the carpet of his deeds to stand naked and shivering before that high Throne whose existence we feel, but cannot see. The fellahin heard various tales about the manner of Sheik Abbas' death; some of them related that the Sheik died insane, while others insisted that disappointment and despair drove him to death by his own hand. But the women who went to offer their sympathies to his wife reported that he died from fear, because the ghost of Samaan Ramy hunted him and drove him every midnight out to the place where Rachel's husband was found slain six years before.

The month of Nisan proclaimed to the villagers the love secrets of Khalil and Miriam. They rejoiced the good tidings which assured them that Khalil would thereby remain in their village. As the news reached all the inhabitants of the huts, they congratulated one another upon Khalil's becoming their beloved neighbour.

When harvest time came, the fellahin went to

the fields and gathered the sheaves of corn and bundles of wheat to the threshing floor. Sheik Abbas was not there to take the crop and have it carried to his bins. Each fellah harvested his own crop; the villagers' huts were filled with wheat and corn; their vessels were replenished with good wine and oil. Khalil shared with them their toils and happiness; he helped them in gathering the crop, pressing the grapes and picking the fruits. He never distinguished himself from any one of them except by his excess of love and ambition. Since that year and up to our present time, each fellah in that village commenced to reap with joy the crop which he sowed with toil and labour. The land which the fellahin tilled and the vineyards they cultivated became their own property.

Now, half a century has passed since this incident, and the Lebanese have awakened.

On his way to the Holy Cedars of Lebanon, a traveller's attention is caught by the beauty of that village, standing like a bride at the side of the valley. The wretched huts are now comfortable and happy homes surrounded by fertile fields and blooming orchards. If you ask any one of the residents about Sheik Abbas' history, he will answer you, pointing with his finger to a heap of demolished stones and destroyed walls saying, "This is the Sheik's palace, and this is the history of his life." And if you inquire about Khalil, he will raise his hand toward heaven saying, "There resides our beloved Khalil, whose life's history was written by God with glittering letters upon the pages of our hearts, and they cannot be effaced by the ages."

END